EVERY CAT

written by Anne W. Phillips
illustrated by Michael Grejniec

HARCOURT BRACE & COMPANY

Orlando Atlanta Austin Boston San Francisco Chicago Dallas New York
Toronto London

Every cat needs a friend
to feed it and give it water.

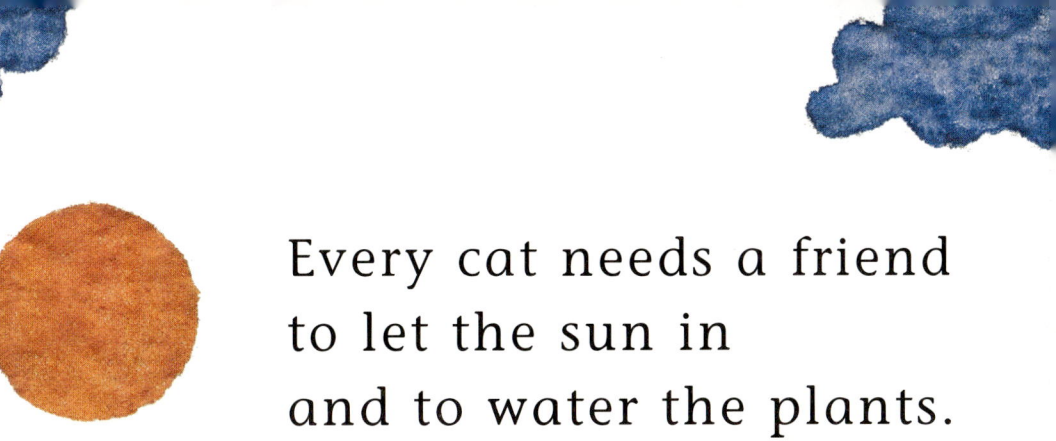

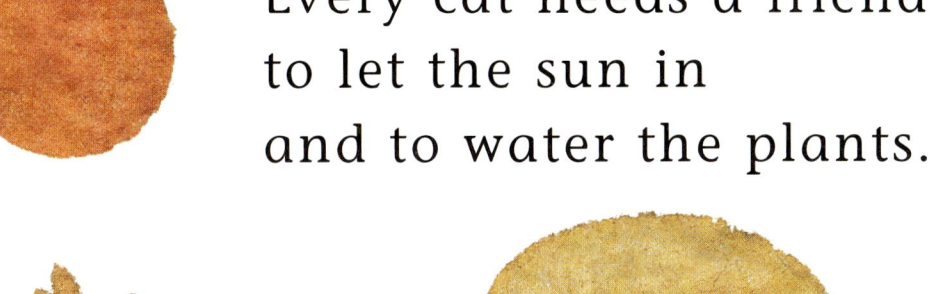

Every cat needs a friend
to let the sun in
and to water the plants.

Every cat needs a friend to help it when it is trapped and scared.

Every cat needs a toy
and a shadow to play with.

Every cat needs a friend
to wait and let it in.

Every cat needs a bed to sleep in and a lap to sit on.

Every pet needs a friend.
Every pet needs someone special.

Is that someone YOU?